DEPARTMENT OF THE TREASURY
TECHNICAL EXPLANATION OF THE PROTOCOL
SIGNED AT HELSINKI ON MAY 31, 2006
AMENDING THE CONVENTION BETWEEN
THE GOVERNMENT OF THE UNITED STATES OF AMERICA
AND
THE GOVERNMENT OF FINLAND
FOR THE AVOIDANCE OF DOUBLE TAXATION AND
THE PREVENTION OF FISCAL EVASION
WITH RESPECT TO TAXES ON INCOME AND ON CAPITAL,
SIGNED AT HELSINKI ON SEPTEMBER 21, 1989

DEPARTMENT OF THE TREASURY
TECHNICAL EXPLANATION OF THE PROTOCOL
SIGNED AT HELSINKI ON MAY 31, 2006
AMENDING THE CONVENTION BETWEEN
THE GOVERNMENT OF THE UNITED STATES OF AMERICA
AND
THE GOVERNMENT OF FINLAND
FOR THE AVOIDANCE OF DOUBLE TAXATION AND
THE PREVENTION OF FISCAL EVASION
WITH RESPECT TO TAXES ON INCOME AND ON CAPITAL,
SIGNED AT HELSINKI ON SEPTEMBER 21, 1989

This is a technical explanation of the Protocol signed at Washington on May 31, 2006 (the "Protocol"), amending the Convention between the United States of America and the Government of Finland for the avoidance of double taxation and the prevention of fiscal evasion with respect to taxes on income, signed at Helsinki on September 21, 1989 (the "Convention").

Negotiations took into account the U.S. Department of the Treasury's current tax treaty policy and Treasury's Model Income Tax Convention, published on September 20, 1996 (the "U.S. Model"). Negotiations also took into account the Model Tax Convention on Income and on Capital, published by the Organization for Economic Cooperation and Development (the "OECD Model"), and recent tax treaties concluded by both countries.

This Technical Explanation is an official guide to the Protocol. It explains policies behind particular provisions, as well as understandings reached during the negotiations with respect to the interpretation and application of the Protocol. This technical explanation is not intended to provide a complete guide to the Convention as amended by the Protocol. To the extent that the Convention has not been amended by the Protocol, the Technical Explanation of the Convention remains the official explanation. References in this technical explanation to "he" or "his" should be read to mean "he or she" or "his or her."

Article I

Article I of the Protocol replaces Article 1 (Personal Scope) of the Convention.

Paragraph 1

Paragraph 1 of Article 1 provides that the Convention applies to residents of the United States or Finland except where the terms of the Convention provide otherwise. Under Article 4 (Residence) of the Convention a person is generally treated as a resident of a Contracting State if that person is, under the laws of that State, liable to tax therein by reason of his domicile, residence, or other similar criteria. However, if a person is considered a resident of both Contracting States, Article 4 provides rules for determining a State of residence (or no State of residence). This determination governs for all purposes of the Convention.

Certain provisions are applicable to persons who may not be residents of either Contracting State. For example, paragraph 1 of Article 24 (Non-Discrimination) applies to nationals of the Contracting States. Under Article 26 (Exchange of Information), information may be exchanged with respect to residents of third states.

Paragraph 2

Paragraph 2 states the generally accepted relationship both between the Convention and domestic law and between the Convention and other agreements between the Contracting States. That is, no provision in the Convention may restrict any exclusion, exemption, deduction, credit or other benefit accorded by the tax laws of the Contracting States, or by any other agreement between the Contracting States. The relationship between the non-discrimination provisions of the Convention and other agreements is addressed not in paragraph 2 but in paragraph 3.

Under paragraph 2, for example, if a deduction would be allowed under the U.S. Internal Revenue Code (the "Code") in computing the U.S. taxable income of a resident of Finland, the deduction also is allowed to that person in computing taxable income under the Convention. Paragraph 2 also means that the Convention may not increase the tax burden on a resident of a Contracting States beyond the burden determined under domestic law. Thus, a right to tax given by the Convention cannot be exercised unless that right also exists under internal law.

It follows that under the principle of paragraph 2 a taxpayer's U.S. tax liability need not be determined under the Convention if the Code would produce a more favorable result. A taxpayer may not, however, choose among the provisions of the Code and the Convention in an inconsistent manner in order to minimize tax. For example, assume that a resident of Finland has three separate businesses in the United States. One is a profitable permanent establishment and the other two are trades or businesses that would earn taxable income under the Code but that do not meet the permanent establishment threshold tests of the Convention. One is profitable and the other incurs a loss. Under the Convention, the income of the permanent establishment is taxable in the United States, and both the profit and loss of the other two businesses are ignored. Under the Code, all three would be subject to tax, but the loss would offset the profits of the two profitable ventures. The taxpayer may not invoke the Convention to exclude the profits of the profitable trade or business and invoke the Code to claim the loss of the loss trade or business against the profit of the permanent establishment. (See Rev. Rul. 84-17, 1984-1 C.B. 308.) If, however, the taxpayer invokes the Code for the taxation of all three ventures, he would not be precluded from invoking the Convention with respect, for example, to any dividend income he may receive from the United States that is not effectively connected with any of his business activities in the United States.

Similarly, nothing in the Convention can be used to deny any benefit granted by any other agreement between the United States and Finland.

Paragraph 3

Paragraph 3 specifically relates to non-discrimination obligations of the Contracting States under the General Agreement on Trade in Services (the "GATS"). The provisions of paragraph 3 are an exception to the rule provided in paragraph 2 of this Article under which the Convention shall not restrict in any manner any benefit now or hereafter accorded by any other agreement between the Contracting States.

Subparagraph (a) of paragraph 3 provides that, unless the competent authorities determine that a taxation measure is not within the scope of the Convention, the national treatment obligations of the GATS shall not apply with respect to that measure. Further, any question arising as to the interpretation of the Convention, including in particular whether a measure is within the scope of the Convention shall be considered only by the competent authorities of the Contracting States, and the procedures under the Convention exclusively shall apply to the dispute. Thus, paragraph 3 of Article XXII (Consultation) of the GATS may not be used to bring a dispute before the World Trade Organization unless the competent authorities of both Contracting States have determined that the relevant taxation measure is not within the scope of Article 24 (Non-Discrimination) of the Convention.

The term "measure" for these purposes is defined broadly in subparagraph (b) of paragraph 3. It would include, for example, a law, regulation, rule, procedure, decision, administrative action or guidance, or any other form of measure.

Paragraph 4

Paragraph 4 contains the traditional saving clause found in U.S. tax treaties. The Contracting States reserve their rights, except as provided in paragraph 5, to tax their residents and citizens as provided in their internal laws, notwithstanding any provisions of the Convention to the contrary. For example, if a resident of Finland performs professional services in the United States and the income from the services is not attributable to a permanent establishment in the United States, Article 7 (Business Profits) would by its terms prevent the United States from taxing the income. If, however, the resident of Finland is also a citizen of the United States, the saving clause permits the United States to include the remuneration in the worldwide income of the citizen and subject it to tax under the normal Code rules (*i.e.*, without regard to Code section 894(a)). However, subparagraph 5(a) of Article 1 preserves the benefits of special foreign tax credit rules applicable to the U.S. taxation of certain U.S. income of its citizens resident in Finland.

For purposes of the saving clause, "residence" is determined under Article 4 (Residence). Thus, an individual who is a resident of the United States under the Code (but not a U.S. citizen) but who is determined to be a resident of Finland under the tie-breaker rules of Article 4 would be subject to U.S. tax only to the extent permitted by the Convention. The United States would not be permitted to apply its statutory rules to that person to the extent the rules are inconsistent with the treaty.

However, the person would be treated as a U.S. resident for U.S. tax purposes other than determining the individual's U.S. tax liability. For example, in determining under Code section 957 whether a foreign corporation is a controlled foreign corporation, shares in that corporation held by the individual would be considered to be held by a U.S. resident. As a result, other U.S. citizens or residents might be deemed to be United States shareholders of a controlled foreign corporation subject to current inclusion of Subpart F income recognized by the corporation. See, Treas. Reg. section 301.7701(b)-7(a)(3).

Under paragraph 4, each Contracting State also reserves its right to tax former citizens and former long-term residents for a period of ten years following the loss of such status. Thus, paragraph 4 allows the United States to tax former U.S. citizens and former U.S. long-term residents in accordance with Section 877 of the Code. Section 877 generally applies to a former citizen or long-term resident of the United States who relinquishes citizenship or terminates long-term residency if either of the following criteria exceed established thresholds: (a) the average annual net income tax of such individual for the period of 5 taxable years ending before the date of the loss of status, or (b) the net worth of such individual as of the date of the loss of status. The average annual net income tax threshold is adjusted annually for inflation. The United States defines "long-term resident" as an individual (other than a U.S. citizen) who is a lawful permanent resident of the United States in at least 8 of the prior 15 taxable years. An individual is not treated as a lawful permanent resident for any taxable year if such individual is treated as a resident of a foreign country under the provisions of a tax treaty between the United States and the foreign country and the individual does not waive the benefits of such treaty applicable to residents of the foreign country.

Paragraph 5

Paragraph 5 sets forth certain exceptions to the application of the saving clause. The referenced provisions are intended to provide benefits to citizens and residents even if such benefits do not exist under internal law. Paragraph 5 thus preserves these benefits for citizens and residents of the Contracting States.

Subparagraph (a) lists certain provisions of the Convention that are applicable to all citizens and residents of a Contracting State, despite the general saving clause rule of paragraph 4:

(1) Paragraph 2 of Article 9 (Associated Enterprises) grants the right to a correlative adjustment with respect to income tax due on profits reallocated under Article 9.

(2) Paragraphs 1 b) and 4 of Article 18 (Pensions, Annuities, Alimony, and Child Support) provide exemptions from source or residence State taxation for certain pension distributions, social security payments and child support.

(3) Article 23 (Elimination of Double Taxation) confirms to citizens and residents of one Contracting State the benefit of a credit for income taxes paid to the other or an exemption for income earned in the other State.

(4) Article 24 (Non-Discrimination) protects residents and nationals of one Contracting State against the adoption of certain discriminatory practices in the other Contracting State.

(5) Article 25 (Mutual Agreement Procedure) confers certain benefits on citizens and residents of the Contracting States in order to reach and implement solutions to disputes between the two Contracting States. For example, the competent authorities are permitted to use a definition of a term that differs from an internal law definition. The statute of limitations may be waived for refunds, so that the benefits of an agreement may be implemented.

Subparagraph (b) of paragraph 5 provides a different set of exceptions to the saving clause. The benefits referred to are all intended to be granted to temporary residents of a Contracting State (for example, in the case of the United States, holders of non-immigrant visas), but not to citizens or to persons who have acquired permanent residence in that State. If beneficiaries of these provisions travel from one of the Contracting States to the other, and remain in the other long enough to become residents under its internal law, but do not acquire permanent residence status (i.e., in the U.S. context, they do not become "green card" holders) and are not citizens of that State, the host State will continue to grant these benefits even if they conflict with the statutory rules. The benefits preserved by this paragraph are the host country exemptions for government service salaries and pensions under Article 19 (Government Service), certain income of visiting students and trainees under Article 20 (Students and Trainees), and the income of diplomatic agents and consular officers under Article 27 (Members of Diplomatic Missions and Consular Posts).

Paragraph 6

Paragraph 6 addresses special issues presented by fiscally transparent entities such as partnerships and certain estates and trusts. Because different countries frequently take different views as to when an entity is fiscally transparent, the risk of both double taxation and double non-taxation are relatively high. The intention of paragraph 6 is to eliminate a number of technical problems that arguably would have prevented investors using such entities from claiming treaty benefits, even though such investors would be subject to tax on the income derived through such entities. The provision also prevents the use of such entities to claim treaty benefits in circumstances where the person investing through such an entity is not subject to tax on the income in its State of residence. The provision, and the corresponding requirements of the substantive rules of Articles 6 through 21, should be read with those two goals in mind.

In general, paragraph 6 relates to entities that are not subject to tax at the entity level, as distinct from entities that are subject to tax, but with respect to which tax may be relieved under an integrated system. This paragraph applies to any resident of a

Contracting State who is entitled to income derived through an entity that is treated as fiscally transparent under the laws of either Contracting State. Entities falling under this description in the United States include partnerships, common investment trusts under section 584 and grantor trusts. This paragraph also applies to U.S. limited liability companies ("LLCs") that are treated as partnerships or as disregarded entities for U.S. tax purposes.

Under paragraph 6, an item of income derived by such a fiscally transparent entity will be considered to be derived by a resident of a Contracting State if a resident is treated under the taxation laws of that State as deriving the item of income. For example, if a Finnish company pays interest to an entity that is treated as fiscally transparent for U.S. tax purposes, the interest will be considered derived by a resident of the U.S. only to the extent that the taxation laws of the United States treat one or more U.S. residents (whose status as U.S. residents is determined, for this purpose, under U.S. tax law) as deriving the interest for U.S. tax purposes. In the case of a partnership, the persons who are, under U.S. tax laws, treated as partners of the entity would normally be the persons whom the U.S. tax laws would treat as deriving the interest income through the partnership. Also, it follows that persons whom the United States treats as partners but who are not U.S. residents for U.S. tax purposes may not claim a benefit for the interest paid to the entity under the Convention, because they are not residents of the United States for purposes of claiming this treaty benefit. (If, however, the country in which they are treated as resident for tax purposes, as determined under the laws of that country, has an income tax convention with Finland, they may be entitled to claim a benefit under that convention.) In contrast, if, for example, an entity is organized under U.S. laws and is classified as a corporation for U.S. tax purposes, interest paid by a Finnish company to the U.S. entity will be considered derived by a resident of the United States since the U.S. corporation is treated under U.S. taxation laws as a resident of the United States and as deriving the income.

The same result obtains even if the entity were viewed differently under the tax laws of the other Contracting State (*e.g.*, as not fiscally transparent in Finland in the first example above where the entity is treated as a partnership for U.S. tax purposes). Similarly, the characterization of the entity in a third country is also irrelevant, even if the entity is organized in that third country. The results follow regardless of whether the entity is disregarded as a separate entity under the laws of one jurisdiction but not the other, such as a single owner entity that is viewed as a branch for U.S. tax purposes and as a corporation for Finnish tax purposes. These results also obtain regardless of where the entity is organized (*i.e.*, in the United States, in Finland, or, as noted above, in a third country).

For example, income from U.S. sources received by an entity organized under the laws of the United States, which is treated for Finnish tax purposes as a corporation and is owned by a shareholder who is a resident of Finland for Finnish tax purposes, is not considered derived by the shareholder of that corporation even if, under the tax laws of the United States, the entity is treated as fiscally transparent. Rather, for purposes of the treaty, the income is treated as derived by the U.S. entity.

These principles also apply to trusts to the extent that they are fiscally transparent in either Contracting State. For example, if X, a resident of Finland, creates a revocable trust in the United States and names persons resident in a third country as the beneficiaries of the trust, the trust's income would be regarded as being derived by a resident of Finland only to the extent that the laws of Finland treat X as deriving the income for tax purposes, perhaps through application of rules similar to the U.S. "grantor trust" rules.

Paragraph 6 is not an exception to the saving clause of paragraph 4. Accordingly, paragraph 6 does not prevent a Contracting State from taxing an entity that is treated as a resident of that State under its tax law. For example, if a U.S. LLC with members who are residents of Finland elects to be taxed as a corporation for U.S. tax purposes, the United States will tax that LLC on its worldwide income on a net basis, without regard to whether Finland views the LLC as fiscally transparent.

Article II

Paragraph a) of Article II of the Protocol replaces paragraph 1 of Article 4 (Residence) of the Convention. The term "resident of a Contracting State" is defined in subparagraph a) of paragraph 1. In general, this definition incorporates the definitions of residence in U.S. and Finnish law by referring to a resident as a person who, under the laws of a Contracting State, is subject to tax therein by reason of his domicile, residence, place of management, place of incorporation or any other similar criterion. Thus, residents of the United States include aliens who are considered U.S. residents under Code section 7701(b). Subparagraph a) of paragraph 1 also specifically includes the two Contracting States, and political subdivisions, statutory bodies and local authorities of the two States, as residents for purposes of the Convention.

Certain entities that are nominally subject to tax but that in practice are rarely required to pay tax also would generally be treated as residents and therefore accorded treaty benefits. For example, a U.S. Regulated Investment Company (RIC) and a U.S. Real Estate Investment Trust (REIT) are residents of the United States for purposes of the treaty. Although the income earned by these entities normally is not subject to U.S. tax in the hands of the entity, they are taxable to the extent that they do not currently distribute their profits, and therefore may be regarded as "liable to tax." They also must satisfy a number of requirements under the Code in order to be entitled to special tax treatment.

A person who is liable to tax in a Contracting State only in respect of income from sources within that State or capital situated therein or of profits attributable to a permanent establishment in that State will not be treated as a resident of that Contracting State for purposes of the Convention. Thus, a consular official of Finland who is posted in the United States, who may be subject to U.S. tax on U.S. source investment income, but is not taxable in the United States on non-U.S. source income (see Code section 7701(b)(5)(B)), would not be considered a resident of the United States for purposes of the Convention. Similarly, an enterprise of Finland with a permanent establishment in the United States is not, by virtue of that permanent establishment, a resident of the United States. The enterprise generally is subject to

U.S. tax only with respect to its income that is attributable to the U.S. permanent establishment, not with respect to its worldwide income, as it would be if it were a U.S. resident.

Subparagraph b) of paragraph 1 contains an exception to the general rule of paragraph 1 a) that residence under internal law also determines residence under the Convention. The exception applies with respect to a U.S. citizen or alien lawfully admitted for permanent residence (*i.e.*, a "green card" holder). Under paragraph 1 a), a person is considered a resident of the United States for purposes of the Convention if he is liable to tax in the United States by reason of citizenship. In addition, aliens admitted to the United States for permanent residence ("green card" holders) qualify as U.S. residents under the first sentence of paragraph 1 because they are taxed by the United States as residents, regardless of where they physically reside.

Paragraph 1 b) provides that a U.S. citizen or green card holder will be treated as a resident of the United States for purposes of the Convention, and, thereby entitled to treaty benefits, only if he has a substantial presence (see section 7701(b)(3)), permanent home or habitual abode in the United States. This rule requires that the U.S. citizen or green card holder have a reasonably strong nexus with the United States.

Thus, for example, an individual resident of Mexico who is a U.S. citizen by birth, or who is a Mexican citizen and holds a U.S. green card, but who, in either case, has never lived in the United States, would not be entitled to benefits under the Convention. However, a U.S. citizen who is transferred to Mexico for two years would be entitled to benefits under the Convention if he maintains a permanent home or habitual abode in the United States.

The fact that a U.S. citizen who does not have close ties to the United States may not be treated as a U.S. resident under the Convention does not alter the application of the saving clause of paragraph 4 of Article 1 (Personal Scope) to that citizen. For example, a U.S. citizen who pursuant to the "citizen/green card holder" rule is not considered to be a resident of the United States still is taxable on his worldwide income under the generally applicable rules of the Code.

Subparagraph c) of paragraph 1 of Article 4 of the Convention provides that certain tax-exempt entities such as pension funds and charitable organizations will be regarded as residents of a Contracting State regardless of whether they are generally liable to income tax in the State where they are established. Subparagraph c) applies to legal persons organized under the laws of a Contracting State and established and maintained in that State to provide pensions or other similar benefits pursuant to a plan, or exclusively for religious, charitable, scientific, artistic, cultural, or educational purposes. Thus, a section 501(c) organization (such as a U.S. charity) that is generally exempt from tax under U.S. law is a resident of the United States for all purposes of the Convention.

Paragraph b) of Article II of the Protocol, which replaces paragraph 3 of Article 4 (Residence) of the Convention, addresses dual-residence issues for persons other than individuals. This provision applies to persons such as trusts, estates, and corporations. If such a person is, under paragraph 1 of Article 4 of the Convention, resident in both Contracting States, the competent authorities shall seek to determine a single State of residence for such person for purposes of the Convention.

If the competent authorities do not reach an agreement on a single State of residence, that person may not claim any benefit accorded to residents of a Contracting State by the Convention. The person may, however, claim any benefits that are not limited to residents, such as those provided by paragraph 1 of Article 24 (Non-Discrimination). Thus, for example, a State cannot discriminate against a dual-resident company.

Dual resident persons also may be treated as a resident of a Contracting State for purposes other than that of obtaining benefits under the Convention. For example, if a dual resident company pays a dividend to a resident of the other Contracting State, the U.S. paying agent would withhold on that dividend at the appropriate treaty rate because reduced withholding is a benefit enjoyed by the resident of the other Contracting State, not by the dual resident company. The dual resident company that paid the dividend would, for this purpose, be treated as a resident of the United States under the Convention. In addition, information relating to dual resident companies can be exchanged under the Convention because, by its terms, Article 26 (Exchange of Information) is not limited to residents of the Contracting States.

Article III

Article III of the Protocol replaces Article 10 (Dividends) of the Convention. Article 10 provides rules for the taxation of dividends paid by a company that is a resident of one Contracting State to a beneficial owner that is a resident of the other Contracting State. The Article provides for full residence country taxation of such dividends and a limited source-State right to tax. Article 10 also provides rules for the imposition of a tax on branch profits by the State of source.

Paragraph 1

The right of a shareholder's country of residence to tax dividends arising in the source country is preserved by paragraph 1, which permits a Contracting State to tax its residents on dividends paid to them by a company that is a resident of the other Contracting State. For dividends from any other source paid to a resident, Article 21 (Other Income) grants the residence country exclusive taxing jurisdiction (other than for dividends attributable to a permanent establishment in the other State).

Paragraph 2

The State of source also may tax dividends beneficially owned by a resident of the other State, subject to the limitations of paragraphs 2 and 3. Paragraph 2 generally limits the rate of withholding tax in the State of source on dividends paid by a company resident in that State to 15 percent of the gross amount of the dividend. If, however, the beneficial owner of the dividend is a company resident in the other State and owns directly shares representing at least 10 percent of the voting power of the company paying the dividend, then the rate of withholding tax in the State of source is limited to 5 percent of the gross amount of the dividend. Shares are considered voting shares if they provide the power to elect, appoint or replace any person vested with the powers ordinarily exercised by the board of directors of a U.S. corporation.

The benefits of paragraph 2 may be granted at the time of payment by means of a reduced rate of withholding tax at source. It also is consistent with the paragraph for tax to be withheld at the time of payment at full statutory rates, and the treaty benefit to be granted by means of a subsequent refund so long as such procedures are applied in a reasonable manner.

The determination of whether the ownership threshold for subparagraph a) of paragraph 2 is met for purposes of the 5 percent maximum rate of withholding tax is made on the date on which entitlement to the dividend is determined. Thus, in the case of a dividend from a U.S. company, the determination of whether the ownership threshold is met generally would be made on the dividend record date.

Paragraph 2 does not affect the taxation of the profits out of which the dividends are paid. The taxation by a Contracting State of the income of its resident companies is governed by the internal law of the Contracting State, subject to the provisions of paragraph 4 of Article 24 (Non-Discrimination).

The term "beneficial owner" is not defined in the Convention, and is, therefore, defined as under the internal law of the country imposing tax (*i.e.*, the source country). The beneficial owner of the dividend for purposes of Article 10 is the person to which the dividend income is attributable for tax purposes under the laws of the source State. Thus, if a dividend paid by a corporation that is a resident of one of the States (as determined under Article 4 (Residence)) is received by a nominee or agent that is a resident of the other State on behalf of a person that is not a resident of that other State, the dividend is not entitled to the benefits of this Article. However, a dividend received by a nominee on behalf of a resident of that other State would be entitled to benefits. These interpretations are confirmed by paragraph 12 of the Commentary to Article 10 of the OECD Model.

Companies holding shares through fiscally transparent entities such as partnerships are considered for purposes of this paragraph to hold their proportionate interest in the shares held by the intermediate entity. As a result, companies holding shares through such entities may be able to claim the benefits of subparagraph (a) under certain circumstances. The lower rate applies when the company's proportionate share of the shares held by the intermediate entity meets the 10 percent threshold, and the company meets the requirements of Article 1(6) (i.e., the company's country of residence treats the intermediate entity as fiscally transparent) with respect to the dividend. Whether this ownership threshold is satisfied may be difficult to determine and often will require an analysis of the partnership or trust agreement.

Paragraph 3

Paragraph 3 provides exclusive residence-country taxation (*i.e.,* an elimination of withholding tax) with respect to certain dividends distributed by a company that is a resident of one Contracting State to a resident of the other Contracting State. As described further below, this elimination of withholding tax is available with respect to certain inter-company dividends and with respect to pension funds.

Subparagraph (a) of paragraph 3 provides for the elimination of withholding tax on dividends beneficially owned by a company that has owned 80 percent or more of the voting power of the company paying the dividend for the 12-month period ending on the date entitlement to the dividend is determined. The determination of whether the beneficial owner of the dividends owns at least 80 percent of the voting power of the paying company is made by taking into account both stock owned directly and stock owned indirectly through one or more residents of either Contracting State.

Eligibility for the elimination of withholding tax provided by subparagraph (a) is subject to additional restrictions based on, but supplementing, the rules of Article 16 (Limitation on Benefits). Accordingly, a company that meets the holding requirements described above will qualify for the benefits of paragraph 3 only if it also: (1) meets the "publicly traded" test of subparagraph 2(c) of Article 16 (Limitation on Benefits), (2) meets the "ownership-base erosion" and "active trade or business" tests described in subparagraph 2(f) and paragraph 4 of Article 16 (Limitation on Benefits), (3) meets the "derivative benefits" test of paragraph 3 of Article 16 (Limitation on Benefits), or (4) is granted the benefits of subparagraph 3(a) of Article 10 by the competent authority of the source State pursuant to paragraph 6 of Article 16 (Limitation on Benefits).

These restrictions are necessary because of the increased pressure on the Limitation on Benefits tests resulting from the fact that the United States has relatively few treaties that provide for such elimination of withholding tax on inter-company dividends. The additional restrictions are intended to prevent companies from re-organizing in order to become eligible for the elimination of withholding tax in circumstances where the Limitation on Benefits provision does not provide sufficient protection against treaty-shopping.

For example, assume that ThirdCo is a company resident in a third country that does not have a tax treaty with the United States providing for the elimination of withholding tax on inter-company dividends. ThirdCo owns directly 100 percent of the issued and outstanding voting stock of USCo, a U.S. company, and of FCo, a Finnish company. FCo is a substantial company that manufactures widgets; USCo distributes those widgets in the United States. If ThirdCo contributes to FCo all the stock of USCo, dividends paid by USCo to FCo would qualify for treaty benefits under the active trade or business test of paragraph 4 of Article 16. However, allowing ThirdCo to qualify for the elimination of withholding tax, which is not available to it under the third state's treaty with the United States (if any), would encourage treaty-shopping.

In order to prevent this type of treaty-shopping, paragraph 3 requires FCo to meet the ownership-base erosion requirements of subparagraph 2(f) of Article 16 in addition to the active trade or business test of paragraph 4 of Article 16. Thus, FCo would not qualify for the exemption from withholding tax unless (i) on at least half the days of the taxable year, at least 50 percent of each class of its shares was owned by persons that are residents of Finland and eligible for treaty benefits under certain specified tests and (ii) less than 50 percent of FCo's gross income is paid in deductible payments to persons that are not residents of either Contracting State eligible for benefits under those specified tests. Because FCo is wholly owned by a third country resident, FCo could not qualify for the elimination of withholding tax on dividends from USCo under the ownership-base erosion test and the active trade or business test. Consequently, FCo would need to qualify under another test or obtain discretionary relief from the competent authority under Article 16(6). For purposes of Article 10(3)(a)(ii), it is not sufficient for a company to qualify for treaty benefits generally under the active trade or business test or the ownership-base erosion test unless it qualifies for treaty benefits under both.

Alternatively, companies that are publicly traded or subsidiaries of publicly-traded companies will generally qualify for the elimination of withholding tax. Thus, a company that is a resident of Finland and that meets the requirements of Article 16(2)(c)(i) or (ii) will be entitled to the elimination of withholding tax, subject to the 12-month holding period requirement of Article 10(3)(a).

In addition, under Article 10(3)(a)(iii), a company that is a resident of a Contracting State may also qualify for the elimination of withholding tax on dividends if it satisfies the derivative benefits test of paragraph 3 of Article 16. Thus, a Finnish company that owns all of the stock of a U.S. corporation may qualify for the elimination of withholding tax if it is wholly-owned, for example, by a U.K., Dutch, Swedish, or Mexican publicly-traded company and the other requirements of the derivative benefits test are met. At this time, ownership by companies that are residents of other European Union, European Economic Area or North American Free Trade Agreement countries would not qualify the Finnish company for benefits under this provision, as the United States does not have treaties that eliminate the withholding tax on inter-company dividends with any other of those countries. If the United States were to enter into such treaties with more of those countries, residents of those countries could then qualify as equivalent beneficiaries for purposes of this provision.

The derivative benefits test may also provide benefits to U.S. companies receiving dividends from Finnish subsidiaries, because of the effect of the Parent-Subsidiary Directive in the European Union. Under that directive, inter-company dividends paid within the European Union are free of withholding tax. Under subparagraph (h) of paragraph 7 of Article 16, that directive will also be taken into account in determining whether the owner of a U.S. company receiving dividends from a Finnish company is an "equivalent beneficiary." Thus, a company that is a resident of a member state of the European Union will, by definition, meet the requirements regarding equivalent benefits with respect to any dividends received by its U.S. subsidiary from a Finnish company. For example, assume USCo is a wholly-owned subsidiary of ICo, an Italian publicly-traded company. USCo owns all of the shares of FCo, a Finnish company. If FCo were to pay dividends directly to ICo, those dividends would be exempt from withholding tax in Finland by reason of the Parent-Subsidiary Directive. If ICo meets the other conditions of subparagraph 7(g) of Article 16, it will be treated as an equivalent beneficiary by reason of subparagraph 7(h) of that article.

A company also may qualify for the elimination of withholding tax pursuant to Article 10(3)(a)(iii) if it is owned by seven or fewer U.S. or Finnish residents who qualify as an "equivalent beneficiary" and meet the other requirements of the derivative benefits provision. This rule may apply, for example, to certain Finnish corporate joint venture vehicles that are closely-held by a few Finnish resident individuals.

Subparagraph g) of paragraph 7 of Article 16 contains a specific rule of application intended to ensure that for purposes of applying Article 10(3) certain joint ventures, not just wholly-owned subsidiaries, can qualify for benefits. For example, assume that the United States were to enter into a treaty with Country X, a member of the European Union, that includes a provision identical to Article 10(3). USCo is 100 percent owned by FCo, a Finnish company, which in turn is owned 49 percent by PCo, a Finnish publicly-traded company, and 51 percent by XCo, a publicly-traded company that is resident in Country X. In the absence of a special rule for interpreting the derivative benefits provision, each of the shareholders would be treated as owning only its proportionate share of the shares held by FCo. If that rule were applied in this situation, neither shareholder would be an equivalent beneficiary, because neither would meet the 80 percent ownership test with respect to USCo. However, since both PCo and XCo are residents of countries that have treaties with the United States that provide for elimination of withholding tax on inter-company dividends, it is appropriate to provide benefits to FCo in this case.

Consequently, when determining whether a person is an equivalent beneficiary under paragraph 7 of Article 16, each of the shareholders is treated as owning shares with the same percentage of voting power as the shares held by FCo for purposes of determining whether it would be entitled to an equivalent rate of withholding tax. This rule is necessary because of the high ownership threshold for qualification for the elimination of withholding tax on inter-company dividends.

If a company does not qualify for the elimination of withholding tax under any of the foregoing objective tests, it may request a determination from the relevant competent authority pursuant to paragraph 6 of Article 16. Benefits will be granted with respect to an item of income if the competent authority of the Contracting State in which the income arises determines that the establishment, acquisition or maintenance of such resident and the conduct of its operations did not have as one of its principal purposes the obtaining of benefits under the Convention.

Subparagraph (b) of paragraph 3 of Article 10 of the Convention provides that dividends beneficially owned by a pension fund (as defined in subparagraph (j) of paragraph 7 of Article 16) may not be taxed in the Contracting State of which the company paying the dividends is a resident, unless such dividends are derived from the carrying on of a business, directly by the pension fund or indirectly through an associated enterprise.

This rule is necessary because pension funds normally do not pay tax (either through a general exemption or because reserves for future pension liabilities effectively offset all of the fund's income), and therefore cannot benefit from a foreign tax credit. Moreover, distributions from a pension fund generally do not maintain the character of the underlying income, so the beneficiaries of the pension are not in a position to claim a foreign tax credit when they finally receive the pension, in many cases years after the withholding tax has been paid. Accordingly, in the absence of this rule, the dividends would almost certainly be subject to unrelieved double taxation.

Paragraph 4

Article 10 generally applies to distributions made by a RIC or a REIT. However, distributions made by a REIT or certain RICs that are attributable to gains derived from the alienation of U.S. real property interests and treated as gain recognized under section 897(h)(1) are taxable under paragraph 1 of Article 13 instead of Article 10. In the case of RIC or REIT distributions to which Article 10 applies, paragraph 4 imposes limitations on the rate reductions provided by paragraphs 2 and 3 in the case of dividends paid by a RIC or a REIT.

The first sentence of subparagraph 4(a) provides that dividends paid by a RIC or REIT are not eligible for the 5 percent rate of withholding tax of subparagraph 2(a) or the elimination of source-country withholding tax of subparagraph 3(a).

The second sentence of subparagraph 4(a) provides that the 15 percent maximum rate of withholding tax of subparagraph 2(b) applies to dividends paid by RICs and that the elimination of source-country withholding tax of subparagraph 3(b) applies to dividends paid by RICs and beneficially owned by a pension fund.

The third sentence of subparagraph 4(a) provides that the 15 percent rate of withholding tax also applies to dividends paid by a REIT and that the elimination of source-country withholding tax of subparagraph 3(b) applies to dividends paid by REITs and beneficially owned by a pension fund, provided that one of the three following conditions is met. First, the beneficial owner of the dividend is an individual or a pension fund, in either case holding an interest of not more than 10 percent in the REIT. Second, the dividend is paid with respect to a class of stock that is publicly traded and the beneficial owner of the dividend is a person holding an interest of not more than 5 percent of any class of the REIT's shares. Third, the beneficial owner of the dividend holds an interest in the REIT of not more than 10 percent and the REIT is "diversified."

Subparagraph (b) provides a definition of the term "diversified," which is necessary because the term is not defined in the Code. A REIT is diversified if the gross value of no single interest in real property held by the REIT exceeds 10 percent of the gross value of the REIT's total interest in real property. Foreclosure property is not considered an interest in real property, and a REIT holding a partnership interest is

14

treated as owning its proportionate share of any interest in real property held by the partnership.

The restrictions set out above are intended to prevent the use of these entities to gain inappropriate U.S. tax benefits. For example, a company resident in Finland that wishes to hold a diversified portfolio of U.S. corporate shares could hold the portfolio directly and would bear a U.S. withholding tax of 15 percent on all of the dividends that it receives. Alternatively, it could hold the same diversified portfolio by purchasing 10 percent or more of the interests in a RIC. If the RIC is a pure conduit, there may be no U.S. tax cost to interposing the RIC in the chain of ownership. Absent the special rule in paragraph 4, such use of the RIC could transform portfolio dividends, taxable in the United States under the Convention at a 15 percent maximum rate of withholding tax, into direct investment dividends taxable at a 5 percent maximum rate of withholding tax or eligible for the elimination of source-country withholding tax.

Similarly, a resident of Finland directly holding U.S. real property would pay U.S. tax on rental income either at a 30 percent rate of withholding tax on the gross income or at graduated rates on the net income. As in the preceding example, by placing the real property in a REIT, the investor could, absent a special rule, transform rental income into dividend income from the REIT, taxable at the rates provided in Article 10, significantly reducing the U.S. tax that otherwise would be imposed. Paragraph 4 prevents this result and thereby avoids a disparity between the taxation of direct real estate investments and real estate investments made through REIT conduits. In the cases in which paragraph 4 allows a dividend from a REIT to be eligible for the 15 percent rate of withholding tax, the holding in the REIT is not considered the equivalent of a direct holding in the underlying real property.

Paragraph 5

Paragraph 5 defines the term "dividends" broadly and flexibly. The definition is intended to cover all arrangements that yield a return on an equity investment in a corporation as determined under the tax law of the state of source, including types of arrangements that might be developed in the future.

The term includes income from shares, or other corporate rights that are not treated as debt under the law of the source State, that participate in the profits of the company. The term also includes income that is subjected to the same tax treatment as income from shares by the law of the State of source. Thus, a constructive dividend that results from a non-arm's length transaction between a corporation and a related party is a dividend. In the case of the United States, the term dividends includes amounts treated as a dividend under U.S. law upon the sale or redemption of shares or upon a transfer of shares in a reorganization. See, *e.g.*, Rev. Rul. 92-85, 1992-2 C.B. 69 (sale of foreign subsidiary's stock to U.S. sister company is a deemed dividend to extent of subsidiary's and sister's earnings and profits). Further, a distribution from a U.S. publicly traded limited partnership, which is taxed as a corporation under U.S. law, is a dividend for purposes of Article 10. However, a distribution by a limited liability company is not taxable by the United States under Article 10, provided the limited liability company is not characterized as an association taxable as a corporation under U.S. law.

Finally, a payment denominated as interest that is made by a thinly capitalized corporation may be treated as a dividend to the extent that the debt is recharacterized as equity under the laws of the source State.

Paragraph 6

Paragraph 6 provides that the general source country limitations under paragraph 2 and 3 on dividends do not apply if the beneficial owner of the dividends carries on business through a permanent establishment situated in the source country, or performs in the source country independent personal services from a fixed base situated therein, and the dividends are attributable to such permanent establishment or fixed base. In such case, the rules of Article 7 (Business Profits) or Article 14 (Independent Personal Services) shall apply, as the case may be. Accordingly, such dividends will be taxed on a net basis using the rates and rules of taxation generally applicable to residents of the Contracting State in which the permanent establishment or fixed base is located, as such rules may be modified by the Convention. An example of dividends attributable to a permanent establishment would be dividends derived by a dealer in stock or securities from stock or securities that the dealer held for sale to customers.

Paragraph 7

The right of a Contracting State to tax dividends paid by a company that is a resident of the other Contracting State is restricted by paragraph 7 to cases in which the dividends are paid to a resident of that Contracting State or are attributable to a permanent establishment or fixed base in that Contracting State. Thus, a Contracting State may not impose a "secondary" withholding tax on dividends paid by a nonresident company out of earnings and profits from that Contracting State. In the case of the United States, the secondary withholding tax was eliminated for payments made after December 31, 2004 in the American Jobs Creation Act of 2004.

Paragraphs 8 and 9

Paragraph 8 permits a Contracting State to impose a branch profits tax on a company resident in the other Contracting State. The tax is in addition to other taxes permitted by the Convention. The term "company" is defined in subparagraph 1(d) of Article 3 (General Definitions).

A Contracting State may impose a branch profits tax on a company if the company has income attributable to a permanent establishment in that Contracting State, derives income from real property in that Contracting State that is taxed on a net basis under Article 6 (Income from Immovable (Real) Property), or realizes gains taxable in that State under paragraph 1 of Article 13 (Gains). In the case of the United States, the imposition of such tax is limited, however, to the portion of the aforementioned items of income that represents the amount of such income that is the "dividend equivalent amount." This is consistent with the relevant rules under the U.S. branch profits tax, and the term dividend equivalent amount is defined under U.S. law. Section 884 defines the dividend equivalent amount as an amount for a particular year that is equivalent to the income described above that is included in the corporation's effectively connected earnings and profits for that year, after payment of the corporate tax under Articles 6 (Income from Immovable (Real) Property), 7 (Business Profits) or 13 (Gains), reduced for any increase in the branch's U.S. net equity during the year or increased for any reduction in its U.S. net equity during the year. U.S. net equity is U.S. assets less U.S. liabilities. See Treas. Reg. section 1.884-1. The dividend equivalent amount for any year approximates the dividend that a U.S. branch office would have paid during the year if the branch had been operated as a separate U.S. subsidiary company.

In Finland, similarly, the imposition of a branch profits tax on business profits attributable to a permanent establishment in Finland, as well as income that is subject to tax under Article 6 (Income from Immovable (Real) Property) or paragraph 1 of Article 13, is limited to amounts, as defined under the laws of Finland, that would be distributed as a dividend if the operation were carried on by a Finnish subsidiary. Although Finland currently does not have statutory provisions for imposition of a branch tax, subparagraph b) of paragraph 8 preserves Finland's right to impose such a tax if one is subsequently enacted, provided that the base of that tax is limited to an amount that is analogous to the dividend equivalent amount.

Paragraph 9 limits the rate of the branch profits tax allowed under paragraph 8 to 5 percent. Paragraph 9 also provides, however, that the branch profits tax will not be imposed if certain requirements are met. In general, these requirements provide rules for a branch that parallel the rules for when a dividend paid by a subsidiary will be subject to exclusive residence-country taxation (i.e., the elimination of source-country withholding tax). Accordingly, the branch profits tax may not be imposed in the case of a company that: (1) meets the "publicly traded" test of subparagraph 2(c) of Article 16 (Limitation of Benefits), (2) meets the "ownership-base erosion" and "active trade or business" tests described in subparagraph 2(f) and subparagraph 4 of Article 16, (3) meets the "derivative benefits" test of paragraph 3 of Article 16, or (4) is granted benefits with respect to the elimination of the branch profits tax by the competent authority pursuant to paragraph 6 of Article 16.

Thus, for example, if a Finnish company would be subject to the branch profits tax with respect to profits attributable to a U.S. branch and not reinvested in that branch, paragraph 9 may apply to eliminate the branch profits tax if the company either met the "publicly traded" test, met the combined "ownership-base erosion" *and* "active trade or business" test, or met the derivative benefits test. If, by contrast, a Finnish company did not meet those tests, but met the ownership-base erosion test (and thus qualified for treaty benefits under subparagraph 2(a)), then the branch profits tax would apply at a rate of 5 percent, unless the Finnish company is granted benefits with respect to the elimination of the branch profits tax by the competent authority pursuant to paragraph 6 of Article 16.

Relation to Other Articles

Notwithstanding the foregoing limitations on source country taxation of dividends, the saving clause of paragraph 4 of Article 1 (Personal Scope) permits the United States to tax dividends received by its residents and citizens as if the Convention had not come into effect.

The benefits of this Article are also subject to the provisions of Article 16 (Limitation on Benefits). Thus, if a resident of Finland is the beneficial owner of dividends paid by a U.S. corporation, the shareholder must qualify for treaty benefits under at least one of the tests of Article 16 in order to receive the benefits of this Article.

Paragraph 2 of Article III of the Protocol makes a conforming change to the cross-reference in paragraph 5 of Article 24 (Non-Discrimination) of the Convention.

Article IV

Article IV of the Protocol modifies Article 11 (Interest) of the Convention by adding a new paragraph 6, providing anti-abuse exceptions to the source-country exemption in paragraph 1 for two classes of interest payments.

The first class of interest, dealt with in subparagraph (a) of paragraph 6, is so-called "contingent interest." Such interest is defined in subparagraph (a) as any interest paid by a resident of a Contracting State that is determined by reference to the receipts, sales, income, profits or other cash flow of the debtor or a related person, to any change in the value of any property of the debtor or a related person or to any dividend, partnership distribution or similar payment made by the debtor or a related person and paid to a resident of the other Contracting State. Any such interest may be taxed in the Contracting State in which it arises according to the laws of that State. If the beneficial owner is a resident of the other Contracting State, however, the gross amount of the interest may be taxed at a rate not exceeding 15 percent.

The second class of interest is dealt with in subparagraph (b) of paragraph 6. This exception is consistent with the policy of Code sections 860E(e) and 860G(b) that excess inclusions with respect to a real estate mortgage investment conduit (REMIC) should bear full U.S. tax in all cases. Without a full tax at source, foreign purchasers of residual interests would have a competitive advantage over U.S. purchasers at the time these interests are initially offered. Also, absent this rule, the U.S. fisc would suffer a revenue loss with respect to mortgages held in a REMIC because of opportunities for tax avoidance created by differences in the timing of taxable and economic income produced by these interests.

Article V

Article V of the Protocol deletes paragraph 2 of Article 12 (Royalties) of the Convention, which allowed taxation in the Contracting State in which they arise of royalties beneficially owned by a resident of the other Contracting State, in the case of payments with respect to certain types of intellectual property. Thus, the change eliminates withholding on cross-border royalty payments regardless of the type of intellectual property involved, bringing the Convention in line with the U.S. Model.

Article VI

Article VI of the Protocol replaces Article 16 (Limitation on Benefits) of the Convention. Article 16 contains anti-treaty-shopping provisions that are intended to prevent residents of third countries from benefiting from what is intended to be a reciprocal agreement between two countries. In general, the provision does not rely on a determination of purpose or intention but instead sets forth a series of objective tests. A resident of a Contracting State that satisfies one of the tests will receive benefits regardless of its motivations in choosing its particular business structure.

The structure of the Article is as follows: Paragraph 1 states the general rule that residents are entitled to benefits otherwise accorded to residents only to the extent provided in the Article. Paragraph 2 lists a series of attributes of a resident of a Contracting State, the presence of any one of which will entitle that person to all the benefits of the Convention. Paragraph 3 provides a so-called "derivative benefits" test under which certain categories of income may qualify for benefits. Paragraph 4 provides that regardless of whether a person qualifies for benefits under paragraph 2 or 3, benefits may be granted to that person with regard to certain income earned in the conduct of an active trade or business. Paragraph 5 provides special rules for so-called "triangular cases" notwithstanding paragraphs 1 through 4 of Article 16. Paragraph 6 provides that benefits may also be granted if the competent authority of the State from which benefits are claimed determines that it is appropriate to grant benefits in that case. Paragraph 7 defines certain terms used in the Article.

Paragraph 1

Paragraph 1 provides that a resident of a Contracting State will be entitled to the benefits of the Convention otherwise accorded to residents of a Contracting State only to the extent provided in this Article. The benefits otherwise accorded to residents under the Convention include all limitations on source-based taxation under Articles 6 through 22, the treaty-based relief from double taxation provided by Article 23 (Elimination of Double Taxation), and the protection afforded to residents of a Contracting State under Article 24 (Non-Discrimination). Some provisions do not require that a person be a resident in order to enjoy the benefits of those provisions. For example, Article 25 (Mutual Agreement Procedure) is not limited to residents of the Contracting States, and Article 27 (Members of Diplomatic Missions and Consular Posts) applies to diplomatic agents or consular officials regardless of residence. Article 16 accordingly does not limit the availability of treaty benefits under such provisions.

Article 16 and the anti-abuse provisions of domestic law complement each other, as Article 16 effectively determines whether an entity has a sufficient nexus to a

Contracting State to be treated as a resident for treaty purposes, while domestic anti-abuse provisions (*e.g.*, business purpose, substance-over-form, step transaction or conduit principles) determine whether a particular transaction should be recast in accordance with its substance. Thus, internal law principles of the source Contracting State may be applied to identify the beneficial owner of an item of income, and Article 16 then will be applied to the beneficial owner to determine if that person is entitled to the benefits of the Convention with respect to such income.

Paragraph 2

Paragraph 2 has six subparagraphs, each of which describes a category of residents that are entitled to all benefits of the Convention.

It is intended that the provisions of paragraph 2 will be self-executing. Unlike the provisions of paragraph 6, discussed below, claiming benefits under paragraph 2 does not require an advance competent authority ruling or approval. The tax authorities may, of course, on review, determine that the taxpayer has improperly interpreted the paragraph and is not entitled to the benefits claimed.

Individuals -- Subparagraph 2(a)

Subparagraph (a) provides that individual residents of a Contracting State will be entitled to all treaty benefits. If such an individual receives income as a nominee on behalf of a third country resident, benefits may be denied under the applicable articles of the Convention by the requirement that the beneficial owner of the income be a resident of a Contracting State.

Governments -- Subparagraph 2(b)

Subparagraph (b) provides that the Contracting States and any political subdivision, statutory body or local authority thereof will be entitled to all the benefits of the Convention. Subparagraph i) of paragraph 7 defines the term "statutory body" to mean any legal entity of a public character created by the laws of a Contracting State in which no person other than the State itself, or a political subdivision or local authority thereof, has an interest. The term "statutory body" was added at Finland's request because under Finnish laws there exist governmental bodies that cannot be properly described as political subdivisions or local authorities. These include, among others, the National Social Insurance Institution, the Bank of Finland (Finland's central bank), and the University of Helsinki.

Publicly-Traded Corporations -- Subparagraph 2(c)(i)

Subparagraph (c) applies to two categories of companies: publicly traded companies and subsidiaries of publicly traded companies. A company resident in a Contracting State is entitled to all the benefits of the Convention under clause (i) of subparagraph (c) if the principal class of its shares, and any disproportionate class of shares, is regularly traded on one or more recognized stock exchanges and the company satisfies at least one of the following additional requirements: first, the company's principal class of shares is primarily traded on a recognized stock exchange located in the Contracting State of which the company is a resident, or, in the case of a company resident in Finland, on a recognized stock exchange located within the European Union, any other European Economic Area country, or, in the case of a company resident in the United States, on a recognized stock exchange located in another state that is a party to the North American Free Trade Agreement; or, second, the company's primary place of management and control is in its State of residence.

The term "recognized stock exchange" is defined in subparagraph (d) of paragraph 7. It includes the NASDAQ System and any stock exchange registered with the Securities and Exchange Commission as a national securities exchange for purposes of the Securities Exchange Act of 1934 and the Helsinki Stock Exchange. The term also includes the Irish Stock Exchange and the stock exchanges of Amsterdam, Brussels, Copenhagen, Frankfurt, London, Oslo, Paris, Reykjavik, Riga, Stockholm, Tallinn, Vilnius, Vienna and Zurich, and any other stock exchange agreed upon by the competent authorities of the Contracting States.

If a company has only one class of shares, it is only necessary to consider whether the shares of that class meet the relevant trading requirements. If the company has more than one class of shares, it is necessary as an initial matter to determine which class or classes constitute the "principal class of shares." The term "principal class of shares" is defined in subparagraph (a) of paragraph 7 to mean the ordinary or common shares of the company representing the majority of the aggregate voting power and value of the company. If the company does not have a class of ordinary or common shares representing the majority of the aggregate voting power and value of the company, then the "principal class of shares" is that class or any combination of classes of shares that represents, in the aggregate, a majority of the voting power and value of the company. Subparagraph (c) of paragraph 7 defines the term "shares" to include depository receipts for shares. Although in a particular case involving a company with several classes of shares it is conceivable that more than one group of classes could be identified that account for more than 50 percent of the shares, it is only necessary for one such group to satisfy the requirements of this subparagraph in order for the company to be entitled to benefits. Benefits would not be denied to the company even if a second, non-qualifying group of shares with more than half of the company's voting power and value could be identified.

A company whose principal class of shares is regularly traded on a recognized stock exchange will nevertheless not qualify for benefits under subparagraph (c) of paragraph 2 if it has a disproportionate class of shares that is not regularly traded on a recognized stock exchange. The term "disproportionate class of shares" is defined in subparagraph (b) of paragraph 7. A company has a disproportionate class of shares if it has outstanding a class of shares that is subject to terms or other arrangements that entitle the holder to a larger portion of the company's income, profit, or gain in the other Contracting State than that to which the holder would be entitled in the absence of such terms or arrangements. Thus, for example, a company resident in Finland meets the test of subparagraph (b) of paragraph 7 if it has outstanding a class of "tracking stock" that pays dividends based upon a formula that approximates the company's return on its assets employed in the United States.

The following example illustrates this result.

Example. FCo is a corporation resident in Finland. FCo has two classes of shares: Common and Preferred. The Common shares are listed and regularly traded on the Helsinki Stock Exchange. The Preferred shares have no voting rights and are entitled to receive dividends equal in amount to interest payments that FCo receives from unrelated borrowers in the United States. The Preferred shares are owned entirely by a single investor that is a resident of a country with which the United States does not have a tax treaty. The Common shares account for more than 50 percent of the value of FCo and for 100 percent of the voting power. Because the owner of the Preferred shares is entitled to receive payments corresponding to the U.S. source interest income earned by FCo, the Preferred shares are a disproportionate class of shares. Because the Preferred shares are not regularly traded on a recognized stock exchange, FCo will not qualify for benefits under subparagraph (c) of paragraph 2.

A class of shares will be "regularly traded" in a taxable year, under subparagraph (e) of paragraph 7, if the aggregate number of shares of that class traded on one or more recognized exchanges during the twelve months ending on the day before the beginning of that taxable year is at least six percent of the average number of shares outstanding in that class during that twelve-month period. For this purpose, if a class of shares was not listed on a recognized stock exchange during this twelve-month period, the class of shares will be treated as regularly traded only if the class meets the aggregate trading requirements for the taxable period in which the income arises. Trading on one or more recognized stock exchanges may be aggregated for purposes of meeting the "regularly traded" standard of subparagraph (e). For example, a U.S. company could satisfy the definition of "regularly traded" through trading, in whole or in part, on a recognized stock exchange located in Finland or certain third countries. Authorized but unissued shares are not considered for purposes of subparagraph (e).

The term "primarily traded" is not defined in the Convention. In accordance with paragraph 2 of Article 3 (General Definitions), this term will have the meaning it has under the laws of the State concerning the taxes to which the Convention applies, generally the source State. In the case of the United States, this term is understood to have the meaning it has under Treas. Reg. section 1.884-5(d)(3), relating to the branch tax provisions of the Code. Accordingly, stock of a corporation is "primarily traded" if the number of shares in the company's principal class of shares that are traded during the taxable year on all recognized stock exchanges in the Contracting State of which the company is a resident exceeds the number of shares in the company's principal class of shares that are traded during that year on established securities markets in any other single foreign country.

A company whose principal class of shares is regularly traded on a recognized exchange but cannot meet the primarily traded test may claim treaty benefits if its primary place of management and control is in its country of residence. This test should be distinguished from the "place of effective management" test which is used in the OECD Model and by many other countries to establish residence. In some cases, the place of effective management test has been interpreted to mean the place where the board of directors meets. By contrast, the primary place of management and control test looks to where day-to-day responsibility for the management of the company (and its subsidiaries) is exercised. The company's primary place of management and control will be located in the State in which the company is a resident only if the executive officers and senior management employees exercise day-to-day responsibility for more of the strategic, financial and operational policy decision making for the company (including direct and indirect subsidiaries) in that State than in the other State or any third state, and the staffs that support the management in making those decisions are also based in that State. Thus, the test looks to the overall activities of the relevant persons to see where those activities are conducted. In most cases, it will be a necessary, but not a sufficient, condition that the headquarters of the company (that is, the place at which the CEO and other top executives normally are based) be located in the Contracting State of which the company is a resident.

To apply the test, it will be necessary to determine which persons are to be considered "executive officers and senior management employees." In most cases, it will not be necessary to look beyond the executives who are members of the Board of Directors (the "inside directors") in the case of a U.S. company. That will not always be the case, however; in fact, the relevant persons may be employees of subsidiaries if those persons make the strategic, financial and operational policy decisions. Moreover, it would be necessary to take into account any special voting arrangements that result in certain board members making certain decisions without the participation of other board members.

<u>Subsidiaries of Publicly-Traded Corporations – Subparagraph 2(c)(ii)</u>

A company resident in a Contracting State is entitled to all the benefits of the Convention under clause (ii) of subparagraph (c) of paragraph 2 if five or fewer publicly traded companies described in clause (i) are the direct or indirect owners of at least 50 percent of the aggregate vote and value of the company's shares (and at least 50 percent of any disproportionate class of shares). If the publicly-traded companies are indirect owners, however, each of the intermediate companies must be a resident of one of the Contracting States.

Thus, for example, a Finnish company, all the shares of which are owned by another Finnish company, would qualify for benefits under the Convention if the principal class of shares (and any disproportionate classes of shares) of the Finnish parent company are regularly and primarily traded on the London stock exchange. However, a Finnish subsidiary would not qualify for benefits under clause (ii) if the publicly traded parent company were a resident of Ireland, for example, and not a resident of the United States or Finland. Furthermore, if a Finnish parent company indirectly owned a Finnish company through a chain of subsidiaries, each such subsidiary in the chain, as an intermediate owner, must be a resident of the United States or Finland for the Finnish subsidiary to meet the test in clause (ii).

Tax-Exempt Organizations -- Subparagraph 2(d)

Subparagraphs 2(d) and 2(e) provide rules by which tax-exempt organizations described in Article 4(1)(c)(i) and pension funds described in paragraph 7(j) of Article 16 will be entitled to all of the benefits of the Convention. A tax-exempt organization other than a tax-exempt pension fund automatically qualifies for benefits, without regard to the residence of its beneficiaries or members. Entities qualifying under this subparagraph are those that are generally exempt from tax in their Contracting State of residence and that are established and maintained exclusively to fulfill religious, charitable, scientific, artistic, cultural, or educational purposes.

Pension Funds -- Subparagraph 2(e)

A pension fund will qualify for benefits if, as of the close of the end of the prior taxable year, more than 50 percent of the beneficiaries, members or participants of the pension are individuals resident in either Contracting State. For purposes of this provision, the term "beneficiaries" should be understood to refer to the persons receiving benefits from the pension fund. "Pension fund" is defined in subparagraph (j) of paragraph 7 to include, in the case of the United States, a tax-exempt pension fund. In the case of Finland, the term "pension fund" includes a pension institution, but if such an institution is organized as a company, only a mutual pension insurance company.

Ownership/Base Erosion -- Subparagraph 2(f)

Subparagraph 2(f) provides an additional method to qualify for treaty benefits that applies to any form of legal entity that is a resident of a Contracting State. The test provided in subparagraph (f), the so-called ownership and base erosion test, is a two-part test. Both prongs of the test must be satisfied for the resident to be entitled to treaty benefits under subparagraph 2(f).

The ownership prong of the test, under clause (i), requires that 50 percent or more of each class of shares or other beneficial interests in the person is owned, directly or indirectly, on at least half the days of the person's taxable year by persons who are residents of the Contracting State of which that person is a resident and that are themselves entitled to treaty benefits under subparagraphs (a), (b), (d), (e) or clause (i) of subparagraph (c) of paragraph 2. In the case of indirect owners, however, each of the intermediate owners must be a resident of that Contracting State.

Trusts may be entitled to benefits under this provision if they are treated as residents under Article 4 (Residence) and they otherwise satisfy the requirements of this subparagraph. For purposes of this subparagraph, the beneficial interests in a trust will be considered to be owned by its beneficiaries in proportion to each beneficiary's actuarial interest in the trust. The interest of a remainder beneficiary will be equal to 100 percent less the aggregate percentages held by income beneficiaries. A beneficiary's interest in a trust will not be considered to be owned by a person entitled to benefits under the other provisions of paragraph 2 if it is not possible to determine the beneficiary's actuarial interest. Consequently, if it is not possible to determine the actuarial interest of the beneficiaries in a trust, the ownership test under clause i) cannot be satisfied, unless all possible beneficiaries are persons entitled to benefits under the other subparagraphs of paragraph 2.

The base erosion prong of clause (ii) of subparagraph (f) is satisfied with respect to a person if less than 50 percent of the person's gross income for the taxable year, as determined under the tax law in the person's State of residence, is paid or accrued, directly or indirectly, to persons who are not residents of either Contracting State entitled to benefits under subparagraphs (a), (b), (d), (e) or clause (i) of subparagraph (c) of paragraph 2, in the form of payments deductible for tax purposes in the payer's State of residence. These amounts do not include arm's-length payments in the ordinary course of business for services or tangible property or payments in respect of financial obligations to a bank that is not related to the payor. To the extent they are deductible from the taxable base, trust distributions are deductible payments. However, depreciation and amortization deductions, which do not represent payments or accruals to other persons, are disregarded for this purpose.

Paragraph 3

Paragraph 3 sets forth a derivative benefits test that is potentially applicable to all treaty benefits, although the test is applied to individual items of income. In general, a derivative benefits test entitles the resident of a Contracting State to treaty benefits if the owner of the resident would have been entitled to the same benefit had the income in question flowed directly to that owner. To qualify under this paragraph, the company must meet an ownership test and a base erosion test.

Subparagraph (a) sets forth the ownership test. Under this test, seven or fewer equivalent beneficiaries must own shares representing at least 95 percent of the aggregate voting power and value of the company and at least 50 percent of any disproportionate class of shares. Ownership may be direct or indirect. The term "equivalent beneficiary" is defined in subparagraph (g) of paragraph 7. This definition may be met in two alternative ways, the first of which has two requirements.

Under the first alternative, a person may be an equivalent beneficiary because it is entitled to equivalent benefits under a treaty between the country of source and the country in which the person is a resident. This alternative has two requirements.

The first requirement is that the person must be a resident of a member state of the European Union, a European Economic Area state, a party to the North American Free Trade Agreement, or Switzerland (collectively, "qualifying States").

The second requirement of the definition of "equivalent beneficiary" is that the person must be entitled to equivalent benefits under an applicable treaty. To satisfy the second requirement, the person must be entitled to all the benefits of a comprehensive treaty between the Contracting State from which benefits of the Convention are claimed and a qualifying State under provisions that are analogous to the rules in paragraph 2 of this Article regarding individuals, governmental entities, publicly-traded companies, and tax-exempt organizations and pensions. If the treaty in question does not have a comprehensive limitation on benefits article, this requirement is met only if the person would be entitled to treaty benefits under the tests in paragraph 2 of this Article applicable to individuals, governmental entities, publicly-traded companies, and tax-exempt organizations and pensions if the person were a resident of one of the Contracting States.

In order to satisfy the second requirement necessary to qualify as an "equivalent beneficiary" under paragraph 7(g)(i)(B) with respect to insurance premiums, dividends, interest, royalties or branch tax, the person must be entitled to a rate of excise, withholding or branch tax that is at least as low as the excise, withholding or branch tax rate that would apply under the Convention to such income. Thus, the rates to be compared are: (1) the rate of tax that the source State would have imposed if a qualified resident of the other Contracting State was the beneficial owner of the income; and (2) the rate of tax that the source State would have imposed if the third State resident received the income directly from the source State. For example, USCo is a wholly owned subsidiary of FCo, a company resident in Finland. FCo is wholly owned by ICo, a corporation resident in Italy. Assuming FCo satisfies the requirements of paragraph 3 of Article 10 (Dividends), FCo would be eligible for the elimination of dividend withholding tax. The dividend withholding tax rate in the treaty between the United States and Italy is 5 percent. Thus, if ICo received the dividend directly from USCo, ICo would have been subject to a 5 percent rate of withholding tax on the dividend. Because ICo would not be entitled to a rate of withholding tax that is at least as low as the rate that would apply under the Convention to such income (*i.e.*, zero), ICo is not an equivalent beneficiary within the meaning of paragraph 7(g)(i) of Article 16 with respect to the elimination of withholding tax on dividends.

Subparagraph 7(h) provides a special rule to take account of the fact that withholding taxes on many inter-company dividends, interest and royalties are exempt within the European Union by reason of various EU directives, rather than by tax treaty. If a U.S. company receives such payments from a Finnish company, and that U.S. company is owned by a company resident in a member state of the European Union that would have qualified for an exemption from withholding tax if it had received the income directly, the parent company will be treated as an equivalent beneficiary. This rule is necessary because many European Union member countries have not re-negotiated their tax treaties to reflect the exemptions available under the directives.

The requirement that a person be entitled to "all the benefits" of a comprehensive tax treaty eliminates those persons that qualify for benefits with respect to only certain types of income. Accordingly, the fact that a French parent of a Finnish company is engaged in the active conduct of a trade or business in France and therefore would be entitled to the benefits of the U.S.-France treaty if it received dividends directly from a U.S. subsidiary of the Finnish company is not sufficient for purposes of this paragraph. Further, the French company cannot be an equivalent beneficiary if it qualifies for benefits only with respect to certain income as a result of a "derivative benefits" provision in the U.S.-France treaty. However, it would be possible to look through the

French company to its parent company to determine whether the parent company is an equivalent beneficiary.

The second alternative for satisfying the "equivalent beneficiary" test is available only to residents of one of the two Contracting States. U.S. or Finnish residents who are eligible for treaty benefits by reason of subparagraphs (a), (b), (c)(i), (d), or (e) of paragraph 2 are equivalent beneficiaries under the second alternative. Thus, a Finnish individual will be an equivalent beneficiary without regard to whether the individual would have been entitled to receive the same benefits if it received the income directly. A resident of a third country cannot qualify for treaty benefits under any of those subparagraphs or any other rule of the treaty, and therefore does not qualify as an equivalent beneficiary under this alternative. Thus, a resident of a third country can be an equivalent beneficiary only if it would have been entitled to equivalent benefits had it received the income directly.

The second alternative was included in order to clarify that ownership by certain residents of a Contracting State would not disqualify a U.S. or Finnish company under this paragraph. Thus, for example, if 90 percent of a Finnish company is owned by five companies that are resident in member states of the European Union who satisfy the requirements of clause (i), and 10 percent of the Finnish company is owned by a U.S. or Finnish individual, then the Finnish company still can satisfy the requirements of subparagraph (a) of paragraph 3.

Subparagraph (b) of paragraph 3 sets forth the base erosion test. A company meets this base erosion test if less than 50 percent of its gross income (as determined in the company's State of residence) for the taxable period is paid or accrued, directly or indirectly, to a person or persons who are not equivalent beneficiaries in the form of payments deductible for tax purposes in company's State of residence. These amounts do not include arm's-length payments in the ordinary course of business for services or tangible property and payments in respect of financial obligations to a bank that is not related to the payor. This test is the same as the base erosion test in clause (ii) of subparagraph (f) of paragraph 2, except that the test in subparagraph 3(b) focuses on base-eroding payments to persons who are not equivalent beneficiaries.

Paragraph 4

Paragraph 4 sets forth an alternative test under which a resident of a Contracting State may receive treaty benefits with respect to certain items of income that are connected to an active trade or business conducted in its State of residence. A resident of a Contracting State may qualify for benefits under paragraph 4 whether or not it also qualifies under paragraphs 2 or 3.

Subparagraph (a) sets forth the general rule that a resident of a Contracting State engaged in the active conduct of a trade or business in that State may obtain the benefits of the Convention with respect to an item of income derived from the other Contracting State. The item of income, however, must be derived in connection with or incidental to that trade or business.

The term "trade or business" is not defined in the Convention. Pursuant to paragraph 2 of Article 3 (General Definitions), when determining whether a resident of Finland is entitled to the benefits of the Convention under paragraph 4 of this Article with respect to an item of income derived from sources within the United States, the United States will ascribe to this term the meaning that it has under the law of the United States. Accordingly, the U.S. competent authority will refer to the regulations issued under section 367(a) for the definition of the term "trade or business." In general, therefore, a trade or business will be considered to be a specific unified group of activities that constitute or could constitute an independent economic enterprise carried on for profit. Furthermore, a corporation generally will be considered to carry on a trade or business only if the officers and employees of the corporation conduct substantial managerial and operational activities.

The business of making or managing investments for the resident's own account will be considered to be a trade or business only when part of banking, insurance or securities activities conducted by a bank, an insurance company, or a registered securities dealer. Such activities conducted by a person other than a bank, insurance company or registered securities dealer will not be considered to be the conduct of an active trade or business, nor would they be considered to be the conduct of an active trade or business if conducted by a bank, insurance company or registered securities dealer but not as part of the company's banking, insurance or dealer business. Because a headquarters operation is in the business of managing investments, a company that functions solely as a headquarters company will not be considered to be engaged in an active trade or business for purposes of paragraph 4.

An item of income is derived in connection with a trade or business if the income-producing activity in the State of source is a line of business that "forms a part of" or is "complementary" to the trade or business conducted in the State of residence by the income recipient.

A business activity generally will be considered to form part of a business activity conducted in the State of source if the two activities involve the design, manufacture or sale of the same products or type of products, or the provision of similar services. The line of business in the State of residence may be upstream, downstream, or parallel to the activity conducted in the State of source. Thus, the line of business may provide inputs for a manufacturing process that occurs in the State of source, may sell the output of that manufacturing process, or simply may sell the same sorts of products that are being sold by the trade or business carried on in the State of source.

Example 1. USCo is a corporation resident in the United States. USCo is engaged in an active manufacturing business in the United States. USCo owns 100 percent of the shares of FCo, a company resident in Finland. FCo distributes USCo products in Finland. Because the business activities conducted by the two corporations involve the same products, FCo's distribution business is considered to form a part of USCo's manufacturing business.

Example 2. The facts are the same as in Example 1, except that USCo does not manufacture. Rather, USCo operates a large research and development facility in the United States that licenses intellectual property to affiliates worldwide, including FCo. FCo and other USCo affiliates then manufacture and market the USCo-designed products in their respective markets. Because the activities conducted by FCo and USCo involve the same product lines, these activities are considered to form a part of the same trade or business.

For two activities to be considered to be "complementary," the activities need not relate to the same types of products or services, but they should be part of the same overall industry and be related in the sense that the success or failure of one activity will tend to result in success or failure for the other. Where more than one trade or business is conducted in the State of source and only one of the trades or businesses forms a part of or is complementary to a trade or business conducted in the State of residence, it is necessary to identify the trade or business to which an item of income is attributable. Royalties generally will be considered to be derived in connection with the trade or business to which the underlying intangible property is attributable. Dividends will be deemed to be derived first out of earnings and profits of the treaty-benefited trade or business, and then out of other earnings and profits. Interest income may be allocated under any reasonable method consistently applied. A method that conforms to U.S. principles for expense allocation will be considered a reasonable method.

Example 3. Americair is a corporation resident in the United States that operates an international airline. FSub is a wholly-owned subsidiary of Americair resident in Finland. FSub operates a chain of hotels in Finland that are located near airports served by Americair flights. Americair frequently sells tour packages that include air travel to Finland and lodging at FSub hotels. Although both companies are engaged in the active conduct of a trade or business, the businesses of operating a chain of hotels and operating an airline are distinct trades or businesses. Therefore FSub's business does not form a part of Americair's business. However, FSub's business is considered to be complementary to Americair's business because they are part of the same overall industry (travel), and the links between their operations tend to make them interdependent.

Example 4. The facts are the same as in Example 3, except that FSub owns an office building in Finland instead of a hotel chain. No part of Americair's business is conducted through the office building. FSub's business is not considered to form a part of or to be complementary to Americair's business. They are engaged in distinct trades or businesses in separate industries, and there is no economic dependence between the two operations.

Example 5. USFlower is a company resident in the United States. USFlower produces and sells flowers in the United States and other countries. USFlower owns all the shares of FHolding, a corporation resident in Finland. FHolding is a holding company that is not engaged in a trade or business. FHolding owns all the shares of three corporations that are resident in Finland: FFlower, FLawn, and FFish. FFlower distributes USFlower flowers under the USFlower trademark in Finland. FLawn markets a line of lawn care products in Finland under the USFlower trademark. In addition to being sold under the same trademark, FLawn and FFlower products are sold in the same stores and sales of each company's products tend to generate increased sales of the other's products. FFish imports fish from the United States and distributes it to fish wholesalers in Finland. For purposes of paragraph 4, the business of FFlower forms a part of the business of USFlower, the business of FLawn is complementary to the business of USFlower, and the business of FFish is neither part of nor complementary to that of USFlower.

An item of income derived from the State of source is "incidental to" the trade or business carried on in the State of residence if production of the item facilitates the conduct of the trade or business in the State of residence. An example of incidental income is the temporary investment of working capital of a person in the State of residence in securities issued by persons in the State of source.

Subparagraph (b) of paragraph 4 states a further condition to the general rule in subparagraph (a) in cases where the trade or business generating the item of income in question is carried on either by the person deriving the income or by any associated enterprises. Subparagraph (b) states that the trade or business carried on in the State of residence, under these circumstances, must be substantial in relation to the activity in the State of source. The substantiality requirement is intended to prevent a narrow case of treaty-shopping abuses in which a company attempts to qualify for benefits by engaging in de minimis connected business activities in the treaty country in which it is resident (*i.e.*, activities that have little economic cost or effect with respect to the company business as a whole).

The determination of substantiality is made based upon all the facts and circumstances and takes into account the comparative sizes of the trades or businesses in each Contracting State, the nature of the activities performed in each Contracting State, and the relative contributions made to that trade or business in each Contracting State. In any case, in making each determination or comparison, due regard will be given to the relative sizes of the U.S. and Finnish economies.

The determination in subparagraph (b) also is made separately for each item of income derived from the State of source. It therefore is possible that a person would be entitled to the benefits of the Convention with respect to one item of income but not with respect to another. If a resident of a Contracting State is entitled to treaty benefits with respect to a particular item of income under paragraph 4, the resident is entitled to all benefits of the Convention insofar as they affect the taxation of that item of income in the State of source.

The application of the substantiality requirement only to income from related parties focuses only on potential abuse cases, and does not hamper certain other kinds of non-abusive activities, even though the income recipient resident in a Contracting State may be very small in relation to the entity generating income in the other Contracting State. For example, if a small U.S. research firm develops a process that it licenses to a very large, unrelated, Finnish pharmaceutical manufacturer, the size of the U.S. research firm would not have to be tested against the size of the Finnish manufacturer. Similarly, a small U.S. bank that makes a loan to a very large unrelated Finnish business would not have to pass a substantiality test to receive treaty benefits under Paragraph 4.

Subparagraph (c) of paragraph 4 provides special attribution rules for purposes of applying the substantive rules of subparagraphs (a) and (b). Thus, these rules apply for purposes of determining whether a person meets the requirement in subparagraph (a) that it be engaged in the active conduct of a trade or business and that the item of income is derived in connection with that active trade or business, and for making the comparison required by the "substantiality" requirement in subparagraph (b). Subparagraph (c) attributes to a person activities conducted by persons "connected" to such person. A person ("X") is connected to another person ("Y") if X possesses 50 percent or more of the beneficial interest in Y (or if Y possesses 50 percent or more of the beneficial interest in X). For this purpose, X is connected to a company if X owns shares representing fifty percent or more of the aggregate voting power and value of the company or fifty percent or more of the beneficial equity interest in the company. X also is connected to Y if a third person possesses fifty percent or more of the beneficial interest in both X and Y. For this purpose, if X or Y is a company, the threshold relationship with respect to such company or companies is fifty percent or more of the aggregate voting power and value or fifty percent or more of the beneficial equity interest. Finally, X is connected to Y if, based upon all the facts and circumstances, X controls Y, Y controls X, or X and Y are controlled by the same person or persons.

Paragraph 5

Paragraph 5 deals with the treatment of insurance premiums, royalties and interest in the context of a so-called "triangular case."

The term "triangular case" refers to the use of the following structure by a resident of Finland to earn, in this case, interest income from the United States. The resident of Finland, who is assumed to qualify for benefits under one or more of the provisions of Article 16 (Limitation on Benefits), sets up a permanent establishment in a third jurisdiction that imposes only a low rate of tax on the income of the permanent establishment. The Finnish resident lends funds into the United States through the permanent establishment. The permanent establishment, despite its third-jurisdiction location, is an integral part of a Finnish resident. Therefore the income that it earns on those loans, absent the provisions of paragraph 5, is entitled to exemption from U.S. withholding tax under the Convention. Under a current Finnish income tax treaty with the host jurisdiction of the permanent establishment, the income of the permanent establishment is exempt from Finnish tax. Thus, the interest income is exempt from U.S. tax, is subject to little tax in the host jurisdiction of the permanent establishment, and is exempt from Finnish tax.

Because the United States does not exempt the profits of a third-jurisdiction permanent establishment of a U.S. resident from U.S. tax, either by statute or by treaty, the paragraph only applies with respect to U.S. source insurance premiums, interest, or royalties that are attributable to a third-jurisdiction permanent establishment of a Finnish resident.

Paragraph 5 replaces the otherwise applicable rules in the Convention for insurance premiums, interest and royalties with a 15 percent withholding tax for interest and royalties and U.S. domestic law rules for insurance premiums if the actual tax paid on the income in the third state is less than 60 percent of the tax that would have been payable in Finland if the income were earned in Finland by the enterprise and were not attributable to the permanent establishment in the third state.

In general, the principles employed under Code section 954(b)(4) will be employed to determine whether the profits are subject to an effective rate of taxation that is above the specified threshold.

Notwithstanding the level of tax on interest and royalty income of the permanent establishment, paragraph 5 will not apply under certain circumstances. In the case of interest (as defined in Article 11 (Interest)), paragraph 5 will not apply if the interest is derived in connection with, or is incidental to, the active conduct of a trade or business carried on by the permanent establishment in the third state. The business of making, managing or simply holding investments is not considered to be an active trade or business, unless these are banking or securities activities carried on by a bank or registered securities dealer. In the case of royalties, paragraph 5 will not apply if the royalties are received as compensation for the use of, or the right to use, intangible property produced or developed by the permanent establishment itself.

Paragraph 6

Paragraph 6 provides that a resident of one of the States that is not entitled to the benefits of the Convention as a result of paragraphs 1 through 5 still may be granted benefits under the Convention at the discretion of the competent authority of the State from which benefits are claimed. In making determinations under paragraph 6, that competent authority will take into account as its guideline whether the establishment, acquisition, or maintenance of the person seeking benefits under the Convention, or the conduct of such person's operations, has or had as one of its principal purposes the obtaining of benefits under the Convention. Benefits will not be granted, however, solely because a company was established prior to the effective date of the Convention or the Protocol. In that case, a company would still be required to establish to the satisfaction of the Competent Authority clear non-tax business reasons for its formation in a Contracting State, or that the allowance of benefits would not otherwise be contrary to the purposes of the Convention. Thus, persons that establish operations in one of the States with a principal purpose of obtaining the benefits of the Convention ordinarily will not be granted relief under paragraph 6.

The competent authority's discretion is quite broad. It may grant all of the benefits of the Convention to the taxpayer making the request, or it may grant only certain benefits. For instance, it may grant benefits only with respect to a particular item of income in a manner similar to paragraph 4. Further, the competent authority may establish conditions, such as setting time limits on the duration of any relief granted.

For purposes of implementing paragraph 6, a taxpayer will be permitted to present his case to the relevant competent authority for an advance determination based on the facts. In these circumstances, it is also expected that if the competent authority determines that benefits are to be allowed, they will be allowed retroactively to the time of entry into force of the relevant treaty provision or the establishment of the structure in question, whichever is later.

A competent authority is required by paragraph 6 to consult the other competent authority before denying benefits under this paragraph.

Paragraph 7

Paragraph 7 defines several key terms for purposes of Article 16. Each of the defined terms is discussed above in the context in which it is used.

Article VII

Paragraph a) amends Article 23 of the convention by deleting paragraph 1) c), which provided that, regardless of any other provision of the Treaty, Finland could tax an individual Finnish national who is a resident of the United States, and who, under Finnish taxation laws, is also a resident of Finland. Due to changes in Finland's domestic tax laws, such a provision is no longer required.

Paragraph b) makes conforming changes to Article 23 to reflect the amendments made to the saving clause of paragraph 4 Article 1 (Personal Scope) and to reflect amendments to section 877 of the Code in 1996.

Paragraph c) amends paragraph 4, which sets forth the source of income rules applicable for purposes of allowing relief under Article 23. Prior to amendment, the source rules of paragraph 4 were subject to such source rules in the domestic laws of the Contracting States as applied for the purpose of limiting the foreign tax credit. Paragraph c) of Article VII of the Protocol removes this limitation in order to ensure that the source rules set out in paragraph 4 of Article 23 have their intended effect.

Article VIII

Article VIII replaces Article 26 (Exchange of Information) of the Convention. This Article provides for the exchange of information and administrative assistance between the competent authorities of the Contracting States.

Paragraph 1

The obligation to obtain and provide information to the other Contracting State is set out in Paragraph 1. The information to be exchanged is that which may be relevant for carrying out the provisions of the Convention or the domestic laws of the United States or Finland concerning taxes of every kind applied at the national level. This language incorporates the standard in 26 U.S.C. section 7602, which authorizes the IRS to examine "any books, papers, records, or other data which may be relevant or material." In United States v. Arthur Young & Co., 465 U.S. 805, 814 (1984), the Supreme Court stated that the language "may be" reflects Congress's express intention to allow the IRS to obtain "items of even potential relevance to an ongoing investigation, without reference to admissibility." However, the language "may be" would not support a request in which a Contracting State simply asked for information regarding all bank accounts maintained by residents of that Contracting State in the other Contracting State, or even all accounts maintained by its residents with respect to a particular bank.

Exchange of information with respect to each State's domestic tax law is authorized to the extent that taxation under domestic tax law is not contrary to the Convention. Thus, for example, information may be exchanged with respect to a covered tax, even if the transaction to which the information relates is a purely domestic transaction in the requesting Contracting State and, therefore, the exchange is not made to carry out the Convention. An example of such a case is provided in the OECD Commentary: a company resident in the United States and a company resident in Finland transact business between themselves through a third-country resident company. Neither Contracting State has a treaty with the third state. To enforce their internal laws with respect to transactions of their residents with the third-country company (since there is no relevant treaty in force), the Contracting States may exchange information regarding the prices that their residents paid in their transactions with the third-country resident.

Paragraph 1 clarifies that information may be exchanged that relates to the assessment or collection of, the enforcement or prosecution in respect of, or the determination of appeals in relation to, the taxes covered by the Convention. Thus, the competent authorities may request and provide information for cases under examination or criminal investigation, in collection, on appeals, or under prosecution.

The taxes covered by the Convention for purposes of this Article constitute a broader category of taxes than those referred to in Article 2 (Taxes Covered). Exchange of information is authorized with respect to taxes of every kind imposed by a Contracting State at the national level. Accordingly, information may be exchanged with respect to U.S. estate and gift taxes, excise taxes or, with respect to Finland, value added taxes.

Information exchange is not restricted by Article 1 (Personal Scope). Accordingly, information may be requested and provided under this article with respect to persons who are not residents of either Contracting State. For example, if a third-country resident has a permanent establishment in Finland, which engages in transactions with a U.S. enterprise, the United States could request information with respect to that permanent establishment, even though the third-country resident is not a resident of either Contracting State. Similarly, if a third-country resident maintains a bank account in Finland, and the Internal Revenue Service has reason to believe that funds in that account should have been reported for U.S. tax purposes but have not been so reported, information can be requested from Finland with respect to that person's account, even though that person is not the taxpayer under examination.

Although the term "United States" does not encompass U.S. possessions for most purposes of the Convention, Section 7651 of the Code authorizes the Internal Revenue Service to utilize the provisions of the Internal Revenue Code to obtain information from the U.S. possessions pursuant to a proper request made under Article 26. If necessary to obtain requested information, the Internal Revenue Service could issue and enforce an administrative summons to the taxpayer, a tax authority (or a government agency in a U.S. possession), or a third party located in a U.S. possession.

Paragraph 2

Paragraph 2 provides that the requesting State may specify the form in which information is to be provided (e.g., depositions of witnesses and authenticated copies of unedited original documents). The intention is to ensure that the information may be introduced as evidence in the judicial proceedings of the requesting State. The requested State should, if possible, provide the information in the form requested to the same extent that it can obtain information in that form under its own laws and administrative practices with respect to its own taxes.

Paragraph 3

Paragraph 3 provides assurances that any information exchanged will be treated as secret, subject to the same disclosure constraints as information obtained under the laws of the requesting Contracting State. Information received may be disclosed only to persons, including courts and administrative bodies, involved in the assessment, collection, or administration of, the enforcement or prosecution in respect of, or the determination of the of appeals in relation to, the taxes covered by the Convention. The information must be used by these persons in connection with the specified functions. Information may also be disclosed to legislative bodies, such as the tax-writing committees of Congress and the Government Accountability Office, engaged in the oversight of the preceding activities. Information received by these bodies must be for use in the performance of their role in overseeing the administration of U.S. tax laws. Information received may be disclosed in public court proceedings or in judicial decisions.

Paragraph 4

Paragraph 4 provides that the obligations undertaken in paragraphs 1 and 3 to exchange information do not require a Contracting State to carry out administrative measures that are at variance with the laws or administrative practice of either Contracting State. Nor is a Contracting State required to supply information not obtainable under the laws or administrative practice of either Contracting State, or to disclose trade secrets or other information, the disclosure of which would be contrary to public policy.

Thus, a requesting Contracting State may be denied information from the other Contracting State if the information would be obtained pursuant to procedures or measures that are broader than those available in the requesting Contracting State.

However, the statute of limitations of the Contracting State making the request for information should govern a request for information. Thus, the Contracting State of which the request is made should attempt to obtain the information even if its own statute of limitations has passed. In many cases, relevant information will still exist in the business records of the taxpayer or a third party, even though it is no longer required to be kept for domestic tax purposes.

While paragraph 4 states conditions under which a Contracting State is not obligated to comply with a request from the other Contracting State for information, the requested State is not precluded from providing such information, and may, at its discretion, do so subject to the limitations of its internal law.

Paragraph 5

Paragraph 5 provides that when information is requested by a Contracting State in accordance with this Article, the other Contracting State is obligated to obtain the requested information as if the tax in question were the tax of the requested State, even if that other State has no direct tax interest in the case to which the request relates. In the absence of such a paragraph, some taxpayers have argued that paragraph 4(a) prevents the requested State from obtaining information from a bank or fiduciary that the requested State does not need for its own tax purposes. This paragraph clarifies that paragraph 4 does not impose such a restriction and that a Contracting State is not limited to providing only the information that it already has in its own files.

Paragraph 6

Paragraph 6 provides that a Contracting State may not decline to provide information because that information is held by financial institutions, nominees or persons acting in an agency or fiduciary capacity. Thus, paragraph 6 would effectively prevent a Contracting State from relying on paragraph 4 to argue that its domestic bank secrecy laws (or similar legislation relating to disclosure of financial information by financial institutions or intermediaries) override its obligation to provide information under paragraph 1. This exception does not include information that would reveal confidential communications between a client and an attorney, solicitor, or other legal representative, where the client seeks legal advice. In the case of the United States, the scope of the privilege for such confidential communications is coextensive with the attorney-client privilege under U.S. law. Paragraph 6 also requires the disclosure of information regarding the beneficial owner of an interest in a person, such as the identity of a beneficial owner of bearer shares.

Paragraph 7

Paragraph 7 provides for assistance in collection of taxes to the extent necessary to ensure that treaty benefits are enjoyed only by persons entitled to those benefits under the terms of the Convention. Under paragraph 7, a Contracting State will endeavor to collect on behalf of the other State only those amounts necessary to ensure that any exemption or reduced rate of tax at source granted under the Convention by that other

State is not enjoyed by persons not entitled to those benefits. For example, if the payer of a U.S.-source portfolio dividend receives a Form W-8BEN or other appropriate documentation from the payee, the withholding agent is permitted to withhold at the portfolio dividend rate of 15 percent. If, however, the addressee is merely acting as a nominee on behalf of a third country resident, paragraph 7 would obligate Finland to withhold and remit to the United States the additional tax that should have been collected by the U.S. withholding agent.

This paragraph also makes clear that the Contracting State asked to collect the tax is not obligated, in the process of providing collection assistance, to carry out administrative measures that are different from those used in the collection of its own taxes, or that would be contrary to its sovereignty, security or public policy.

Effective dates and termination in relation to exchange of information

Once the Protocol is in force, the competent authority may seek information under Article 26 as amended by the Protocol with respect to a year prior to the entry into force of the Protocol, even if Article 26 of the Convention prior to its amendment by the Protocol was in effect during the years in which the transaction at issue occurred.

A tax administration may also seek information with respect to a year for which a treaty was in force after the treaty has been terminated. In such a case the ability of the other tax administration to act is limited. The treaty no longer provides authority for the tax administrations to exchange confidential information. They may only exchange information pursuant to domestic law or other international agreement or arrangement.

Article VIII

Article VIII of the Protocol contains the rules for bringing the Protocol into force and giving effect to its provisions.

Paragraph 1 provides for the ratification of the Convention by both Contracting States and the exchange of instruments of ratification as soon as possible thereafter. The Protocol shall enter into force upon the exchange of instruments of ratification.

In the United States, the process leading to ratification and entry into force is as follows: Once a protocol or treaty has been signed by authorized representatives of the two Contracting States, the Department of State sends the protocol or treaty to the President who formally transmits it to the Senate for its advice and consent to ratification, which requires approval by two-thirds of the Senators present and voting. Prior to this vote, however, it generally has been the practice of the Senate Committee on Foreign Relations to hold hearings on the protocol or treaty and make a recommendation regarding its approval to the full Senate. Both Government and private sector witnesses may testify at these hearings. After the Senate gives its advice and consent to ratification of the protocol or treaty, an instrument of ratification is drafted for the President's signature. The President's signature completes the process in the United States.

The date on which a treaty enters into force is not necessarily the date on which its provisions take effect. Paragraph 2 contains rules that determine when the provisions of the treaty will have effect.

Under subparagraphs (a)(i) and (b)(i), the provisions of the Protocol relating to taxes withheld at source will have effect with respect to amounts paid or credited (or in the case of Finland, income derived) on or after the first day of the second month next following the date on which the Protocol enters into force. For example, if instruments of ratification are exchanged on April 25 of a given year, the withholding rates specified in paragraph 2 of Article 10 (Dividends) would be applicable to any dividends paid or credited on or after June 1 of that year. Similarly, the revised Limitation on Benefits provisions of Article VI of the Protocol would apply with respect to any payments of interest, royalties or other amounts on which withholding would apply under the Code if those amounts are paid or credited on or after June 1.

This rule allows the benefits of the withholding reductions to be put into effect as soon as possible, without waiting until the following year. The delay of one to two months is required to allow sufficient time for withholding agents to be informed about the change in withholding rates. If for some reason a withholding agent withholds at a higher rate than that provided by the Convention (perhaps because it was not able to re-program its computers before the payment is made), a beneficial owner of the income that is a resident of Finland may make a claim for refund pursuant to section 1464 of the Code.

For all other taxes, subparagraphs (a)(ii) and (b)(ii) specify that the Protocol will have effect for any taxable period beginning on or after January 1 of the year next following entry into force.

In both Contracting States, provisions of the Protocol relating to taxes withheld at source covered by paragraph 3 of Article 10 (Dividends) will have effect with respect to income derived on or after January 1, 2007, provided that the Protocol enters into force before December 31, 2007. The relevant date for this purpose is the date on which income from the dividend is derived by the beneficial owner, rather than to the date on which the income was originally derived by the company paying the dividend. The phrase "income derived" was used because it is compatible with the standard for inclusion of income under Finnish tax law. It is intended to have a meaning similar to the phrase "income paid or credited," a standard more commonly used in U.S. tax treaties. Thus, provided the Protocol enters into force prior to December 31, 2007, the provisions of the Protocol eliminating withholding on companies and pension funds meeting the requirement of paragraph 3 of Article 10 (Dividends) will have effect with respect to income derived from dividends paid or accrued on or after January 1, 2007.